Rewrite your Story

IBIYEMI IFEDERU

No part of this book may be reproduced or transmitted in any form or by any means, graphic, electronic, or mechanical, including photocopying, recording, taping or by any information storage or retrieval system, without the permission in writing from the author.

REWRITE YOUR STORY
ISBN: 978-1-912896-00-4
Copyright © January 2019 by Ibiyemi Ifederu
All Rights Reserved

Published in the United Kingdom by

**Syncterface Media
London**

www.syncterfacemedia.com
info@syncterfacemedia.com

Cover Design by Syncterface Media

Acknowledgments

I could not have completed this book without the unwavering support of my husband and best friend. You are my biggest cheerleader and burden bearer.

To my mentor, Sola Oshinoiki whose invaluable support has been constant in my life.

To Jimi Tewe, my dear friend who started it all when he threw me into the deep end of public speaking.

To Elizabeth Adegbiji – your infectious positivity and encouragement was a source of motivation.

To Olawunmi Brigue – you took the script to another level and connected the dots which gave me the impetuous to persevere in the face of despair.

To Akin Akinyemi and the entire team at Syncterface Media – you were the last piece that completed the puzzle. Your dedication to this project is humbling.

To Fiyinfoluwa Taiwo – you are a true gem and you remind me of my younger self. I am privileged to have you in my life.

To my daughter, Grace – thank you for cooperating with me, and allowing me to have a conducive environment to write this book during the first few months of your birth.

To my mum and siblings – you are instrumental

towards the person that I have become. I couldn't thank you enough for your presence in my life.

To my dear friend, Dola Odulaja – this acknowledgement would be incomplete without you.

Finally, to the source of my existence and the inspiration behind this book – Almighty God. It all started with you. This book is in appreciation of you.

Contents

Foreword v

A Word from the Author 1

Making Sense of My Early Life 5

Using Education as a Springboard 11

Climbing the UK Corporate Ladder 15

Crossing the QLTT Hurdle 21

Launching into the Next Level 25

Success is Repeatable 31

About Part II 37

The Image Inside You is Everything 39

Sharpen Your Focus 41

Have Values 45

Manage Time Well 47

Is Your Mind Set? 49

Is Brand "You" Intact? 53

Discipline 57

Don't Confuse Your Personality With Your Behaviour 61

Competency: The Core of Success 65

Success: Myth or Reality 69

About Part III 73

Have You Met "You"? 75

Who Influences You? 79

Do You Understand
Ambition and Goals? 81

About Part IV 89

Foreword

Ibiyemi's life has always been a story of courage and hope and I am glad she has penned this book.

In *Rewrite Your Story*, Ibiyemi chronicles her story of faith and how she wedded marketplace excellence with spiritual maturity. As you read her story, you will grow in faith and expectation of what God can do in your own life. Ibiyemi does not hide her struggles and the difficult decisions she had to make. Her life is fully of her determination and reflections of an entrepreneurial spirit.

This book is not just a testimony of a life impacted, but it challenges us to follow our dreams. It is a book that will shake you out of any form of complacency and fear and enable you to see how God makes ways in the wilderness and brings ideas that we may have been given up to life. Amazing things happen when we pursue God's plans for our lives.

This book is a roadmap to a life fully lived out for God in the marketplace under the shadow of God's wings. Ibiyemi takes you on a journey from her early years to the present day then gives us principles, tools and strategies to achieve success in our careers in the marketplace. Her personal story gives us hope and the ability to dream and imagine a better tomorrow today!

Ibiyemi has pushed on many doors but, it was her faith, hard work, courage, bravery and her unending desire not to give up and settle for less that has got her to where she is now. She shares her techniques for success in a practical, actionable plan as she asks us questions we really want to ask ourselves.

~ Sola Osinoiki ~

Senior Director, People Technology, Naspers

PART I

From Immigrant to Senior Business Leader

1

A Word from the Author

As a young girl living in Lagos Nigeria, I had big dreams and goals that I believed would shape my future. I wanted to relocate to the United Kingdom to follow my dream of becoming a Chartered Secretary. I was no different from the many young and intelligent people with promising futures that I speak with today. Many want to make an impact in life but very palpable in their voices is the despair and frustration they face in what they consider to be unsatisfactory career progression. I empathise with them because I had precisely the same feelings many years back when I started my journey.

It's deeply dissatisfying to have strong desires and ambitions that continuously seem elusive and just out of reach. Further complicating this position is the well-meaning, yet unproductive and demotivating, advice we sometimes receive from people, including those close to us. I remember a good friend telling me, "Ibiyemi, I value you as a person but it appears you are self-deluded!" The rationale behind this comment was rooted in the fact that some research had suggested that eighty-percent of people who relocate to western countries in pursuit of their dreams end up with disappointing outcomes. To him, my expectations of becoming a fully qualified and successful solicitor and chatered secretary in the United Kingdom were too high, and I was setting myself up for failure.

Ten years on, I had become a respected senior chartered secretary in a global telecommunications company, and I was overseeing corporate legal actions and company secretarial matters in the United Kingdom and Europe. Even though I did not obtain a first-class law degree from an Ivy League university, my accomplishments in the United Kingdom have far exceeded the expectations of my peers and of my family.

Thinking about my journey, I could not help but think about others in the same situation but whose potential may be limited by statistics that don't need to represent the ceiling on achieving their goals. As I thought about writing my story, I had a sense of self-doubt. I asked myself a million times why anyone would be interested in what I had to say. Why would anyone want to listen to me? Whenever these self-defeating thoughts arose, I would come across someone who was inspired by what I had achieved and eager for me to share these useful tips on career progression.

I share my story and my experiences with a deep sense of gratitude, honour and hope. Hope that my words will encourage and inspire you to take meaningful action. Hope that my story reinforces your commitment to success and perseverance, knowing that light always breaks at the end of the tunnel. Hope that one day, you dream will become your reality and your story will be an inspiration that will propel others to achieve their goals.

2

Making Sense of My Early Life

My childhood, although privileged, was bittersweet. I was born and raised in Nigeria, a highly-populated country in West Africa. My family was not the typical husband and wife family. In Nigeria, it is not uncommon for a man to have one legal wife and other customary wives as local traditions supported the idea of polygamy. Our family was polygamous and my mother, one of the customary wives, had five children. I was the third child. My Father lived with his first wife and housed his other families in separate locations across the city of Lagos where we lived. Despite this, we were well catered for. My Father often visited with lavish gifts and treats. He could afford any luxury we wanted.

From an early age, I found myself discontented with most things people around me were happy to accept. I disliked any expression of mediocrity and habitually challenged the status quo. I am not quite sure how I managed to combine being reserved and quiet with the strong will that I possessed. Although I lacked nothing materially, I had some unique incidents that, I believe, were contributors to shaping my character as a survivor.

Nigeria has had a long history of political instability that led to military interference in the normal lives of the citizens. Protests and riots were widespread. During one of such uprisings, when I was only about a year old, soldiers, in a bid to disperse mobs, launched tear gas canisters. One of these canisters flew through an open window into the room while I slept and the rest of the family were in the living room. Without knowing what was happening, my mum just had a sudden urge to check on me and found the room engulfed in tear-gas. So overwhelming was the gas that my mum almost fell over. She had to crawl to reach me on the bed. I believe that it was only through the divine intervention of God that I survived the ordeal.

My father passed away when I was five years old. Although I have very few memories of him and barely understood the implications of his death at the time, I remember the details of that period vividly. There were lots of visitors to the house, from family members to close friends and colleagues of my mum. It was a very sober atmosphere. Even though my mum tried to conceal her grief from us, her listless gaze and emaciated frame said it all. My mother was the last of my father's wives and had suddenly been made a widow at the youthful age of thirty-five. Her dream of a long-lasting marriage had been snatched away, and she was left to raise five children by herself.

After the funeral that lasted an entire week, we began a new phase of life without a father. At the time, local customs and traditions were generally unfavourable towards widows. My mum suffered much opposition from my father's relatives who were determined to seize his estate despite the presence of a will. Some even went as far as making unfounded accusations about her involvement in my father's death. She was ostracised and punished for sins she did not commit. In the midst of her grief and struggle to come to terms with her husband's death, she had to fight tooth and nail to secure our financial future.

Barely a year after my father's death, my younger siblings and I suddenly fell ill after returning home from a holiday at my aunty's in Ibadan, a city in the western part of Nigeria. Initially, it was assumed to be a mild fever. However, after a series of tests my brother and I were diagnosed with typhoid fever and my younger sister with meningitis. Typhoid fever was a relatively new disease at the time. My brother and I were among the first few cases to be diagnosed. We spent months in the hospital as the host of doctors and other medical personnel experimented with all kinds of treatments. My time at the hospital felt so long that I wondered if I would ever be well enough to resume life as normal. One person that kept me going was my mother. Her gentle strength and tenacity even in the exceedingly bleak and hopeless situation gave me the daily strength to live for another day.

After spending almost four months in the hospital, my brother and I were well enough to be discharged and complete the final phase of our recovery at home. I was grateful to be home, and life held a new meaning for me, given the close shave I had just had with death. What I did not know was that my sister had devastatingly lost her battle with meningitis. She died at the tender age of seven. My sister and I had been very close, inseparable even, and my mother treated us like twins. My family was afraid of the impact her death would have on me and chose not to break the news to me. They told me she had been transferred to a hospital in the United States for further treatment and would be away for a long time.

Integrating back into normal life without my sister proved very challenging. I missed her so dearly, but for some reason, I chose not to pester my mum with questions about her return. I felt that with all that she had gone through over the past months, she had enough on her plate. A part of me was crying out loud for help, but I kept it all bottled up inside.

After two years without a single update about my sister, I began to secretly concoct a plan to go to the United States so that I could see my sister again. You can imagine the horror on my mother's face when I finally told her my plan. Hearing me say those words deeply affected her and she relented by telling me the truth about my sister. Looking back, I am amazed at her strength and bravery in dealing with the deaths of my father and my sister. She is indeed an extraordinary woman.

I remember the numbness I felt hearing the news of

my sister's death. I had lived in hope and imagined my sister having a wonderful time in the United States, occasionally, wondering if she missed me. My world shattered from the realisation that I would never see her again. A myriad of emotions and questions flooded my mind, but I struggled to find the words to express them the way I desperately wanted to. My sister had been my best friend and confidant. She had stuck up for me even when she knew I was in the wrong. She had been the gentlest of persons with a beautiful soul. Her death made me feel unworthy and guilty. I felt as if I didn't deserve to live, knowing that she was a better person than I was and we had both fought for our lives. I felt like a part of me had been taken away without my consent, yet I had no one to confront or challenge about it. After this experience, I withdrew into my shell and became even quieter.

3

Using Education as a Springboard

Returning to school after my sister's death was a painful experience. Many landmarks brought memories of her back. Even though I looked fine outwardly, I was an emotional wreck. I tried my best in school to focus on my studies, but my grades steadily declined. I was very fortunate to pass the secondary school entrance examination and gain admission into a reputable school.

With the move to secondary school, my focus on my studies improved and so did my grades. I eventually gained admission into one of the top universities in Nigeria at the time. University opened a new and exciting chapter in my life. Because of the life-threatening incident with typhoid fever, my mum did not allow my brother and I to live from home or to attend boarding school, so I had not lived outside of the house in a very long time. I was excited about the liberty and independence university life would bring. It didn't take too long, however, for me to realise that independence came at a price. Without the consistent monitoring and oversight my mother provided when I lived at home, I found myself distracted by the many activities that life on campus afforded. I neglected my studies and waited until the last minute to prepare for examinations. As can be expected, I ended up being overwhelmed by the volume of studying I had to do, and my grades suffered as a result. They were barely average. After a while, I became despondent and stopped striving to excel in my studies.

In my fourth year, I found new inspiration to excel and doubled up on my efforts. The progress I made in that short time allowed me to obtain my LL.B. with a second class lower division (2:2).

Law school

My experience in Law School was different from my time at university. The environment was more serene, probably because it was a postgraduate school exclusively for lawyers. The learning experience was more holistic and focused. Most of my friends from university had been posted to different law schools, so I had to make new friends in law school. I found this to be a good thing because I formed lasting friendships there.

As part of the course, I was posted to a high-profile law office in Lagos to complete a mandatory work experience program. I remember completely immersing myself in a two-day crash course on driving because I was determined to drive myself to the law office and the courthouse. I was terrified when I first set out onto the chaotic Lagos roads and traffic on my own, but by the end of the first week, I was an old pro. This experience taught me that with focus and determination we can achieve a lot more than we imagine.

Work Experience

During my work experience, I was paired with a senior lawyer in the corporate department, who gave me my first insight into the practical aspects of commercial and corporate law. I found myself constantly intrigued and stimulated by the involved transactions and the interactions with the clients. I was fascinated by how companies were controlled and board decisions were made. This experience sparked my interest in corporate law, and by the time I graduated from law school, I had made up my mind to specialise in that field.

After my graduation, I started seriously looking into career opportunities outside Nigeria. I very quickly decided against pursuing a Master's degree in law (L.L.M.), even though it seemed the logical next step. I had a strong desire to be an influential member of an organisation. I wanted to be in the boardroom, where crucial decisions that drive organisations are made. I started to inquire about how to get on the board of an organisation, and I came across the role of the company secretary. I was very excited by this information and the more I researched it, the more it crystallised in my mind that it was the most suitable route to the boardroom.

With my sights fully set on becoming a company secretary, my immediate goals were to join the Institute of Chartered Secretaries and Administrators (ICSA) and take the professional qualification examinations. This led me to the United Kingdom, a destination that particularly appealed to me because of my long-standing relationship with the country. I had family there and had previously, visited several times.

Within eight years, I had become the legal counsel and company secretary for the UK arm of one of the largest global telecommunications companies in the world. When I was interviewed for this role, one of the interviewers made a comment I will never forget. "This lady sounds too good to be true. I won't be surprised if she is promoted within two years of joining us, or even gets poached by another organisation." And, he was right! I was promoted within a year of joining the business.

I have since, throughout my career, gone on to achieve several milestones such as this. I sit on the board of a global organisation; I have spoken at events facilitated by prestigious organisations and business schools including the Henley Business School, alongside respected colleagues in my profession, but I never do I take any of these achievements for granted, because my life has not always been littered with success. My beginnings were distinctly different from what my life looks like now.

4

Climbing the UK Corporate Ladder

*A*rriving in the U.K., many people were keen to tell me that Nigerians lawyers who immigrated to the country usually specialised in immigration law. While I have no objection to Immigration Law, I was clear in my mind that it was not for me. I had a well-formed image of myself, as a key influencer, in the boardroom.

My law degree proved to be an advantage that exempted me from the first three stages of the ICSA qualification. As I studied for the qualification exams, I would, several times, flip through the recruitment section of the ICSA magazine during lecture breaks. The positions advertised were so distinguished that there were moments when I did not consider myself worthy of them, but my fervent desire kept me going.

After completing some of the modules, I started, actively searching, for company secretarial roles.

I landed my first job as a maternity cover for a company secretarial assistant. As a qualified lawyer, I was overqualified for the role, but I considered it a small price to pay for a foothold in that field.

Despite being overqualified, I was still fortunate to get the job because I had no company secretarial experience and I was not a perfect fit for person specification requirements for the role, but I expressed my willingness to learn and develop myself. My passion and enthusiasm must have come across convincingly.

The role was with a large financial services provider. I reported to the Group Company Secretary who was not a solicitor, but I respected her and worked diligently as part of a team. Shortly after I started, I decided to take on a Due Diligence project that was beyond the requirements of my job. During the project, there were several times when I stayed behind after working hours and was often the only one left in the office. During those late nights, I would, sometimes, question the value of investing so much time and effort into the project. However, the knowledge and experience I was gaining kept me going until I completed it.

At the end of my fixed-term tenure, I moved on to a smaller company that provided secretarial services to companies all over the world. I took this role to maintain the momentum I had begun to build in the company secretarial sector. I did not allow the lure of better paying or more prestigious jobs, in other sectors, to take me off the path I had mapped out for myself. The work mainly required the use of a business system to deliver company secretarial support to over 4000 companies across the globe. I knew my time at that company would be short, so I set out to become proficient in the business system so I could add it to my list of skills. At the end of my time at this company, I had acquired enough U.K. experience to start applying for the more strategic roles I really wanted.

I moved to a large asset management firm with a property portfolio of over £2billion, where I was employed as company secretary to provide company secretarial support to the company and its subsidiaries – this was my first opportunity at mid-level management.

I recall my interview vividly. The panel was made up of two people, the Head of Legal and the Finance Director. I gave it my best shot because I was determined to impress the interviewers with everything I had. During the meeting, I confidently painted a compelling picture of my capabilities and prospects, and what I would accomplish if given the opportunity. This was easy to do because I had spent time building a clear and striking internal image of my true identity and where I wanted to be in my career. I undoubtedly saw myself in the boardroom of a large organisation, confidently supporting its directors with their decision-making.

As I had desired, the work was much more strategic and involved core company secretarial duties that allowed me to put to practice the skills I had acquired through my academic training.

The role was a big career break for me. I was finally going to be in the boardroom as a company secretary! It was a memorable highlight in my career. I had created high expectations of my capabilities during the interview, and I was determined to fulfil them. I always updated myself on the technical aspects of my discipline and prepared extensively for board meetings and upcoming projects. Due to the nature of the business, I had to develop a robust understanding of commercial property, including the concepts and terminology used in the sector. The leasing team I worked with was notorious for their cutthroat approach to deal-making, and they were not prepared to wait around for me to get up to speed. There were times when I felt intimidated by some members of the team, but I never allowed it to show. I dedicated long hours in and out of work to learning as much as I could, as fast as I could.

My line manager had limited knowledge of my field and deferred to me often, which I was grateful for. His amiable nature and "hands-off" management style significantly increased my confidence and willingness to perform even better. He would always put in a good word and stand up for me. For example, he orchestrated the approval of the company to sponsor the last few modules of my ICSA qualification. I qualified as a company secretary during my time there.

At another time, a few years into my working in this organisation, the company and its joint-venture partners decided to sell off three out of the seven designer outlet malls they managed at the time. Consequently, about forty percent of my work was to be transferred as part of the sale and I was at serious risk of redundancy. My manager put forward a business case to promote me by combining my company secretarial role with commercial property transactions. This led to me becoming a legal adviser, as well as company secretary at the organisation. I was overwhelmed by the lengths he went to in building a business case for his proposal, and I was genuinely grateful for it. His actions went a long way in recognising my hard work and making me feel valued.

The promotion provided a springboard for my application to become a qualified solicitor in the UK. I received full support from my manager who was also planning to become a qualified solicitor at the time, though via another route. I registered with the Solicitors Regulation Authority (SRA) and enrolled for the Qualified Lawyers Transfer Test (QLTT). I learned very quickly that the timing of the QLTT examinations coincided with my quarterly board meetings. I struggled with the conflict of interests for about a year, trying to fit both in. Despite my efforts, I could not make significant headway in the QLTT while serving as the company secretary at my organisation. I finally accepted that something had to give. So, I decided to quit my job! I wrestled with what I considered the herculean task of breaking the news to my manager, whom I had developed a good working relationship with. I knew my decision to quit would have a massive impact on him.

As expected, he was shocked by the news. He refused to accept my resignation letter and gave me two weeks to rethink my decision. Yet, the more

I thought about it, the more resolute I became. I realised that I had settled into my comfort zone. The work no longer challenged me mentally and there were restricted opportunities for career progression. During this time, I reduced my social activities and kept my decision to myself. I was in a delicate state and did not want the influence of family and friends to sway my resolve. Many people would have considered my decision irresponsible, given the wider implications of being out of a job. There was a lot of uncertainty in the U.K. job market at the time, and many people I knew were unwilling to take the plunge into the adventurous world of the unknown. Nevertheless, my radical desire to pursue my ambition was unflinching. So, I shut my eyes and mind to any thought of failure and focused only on the reasons that supported my decision. Fortunately, I had an ally in my local Pastor who chose to support me and encouraged me to follow my heart.

I reiterated my decision to resign to my manager, which he reluctantly accepted. In the weeks prior, I had created a process document for the work I did as company secretary to alleviate the impact my resignation would have on my manager and the company as a whole. He was very impressed by this gesture and viewed it as a welcome compromise. I believe he was truly happy for me and supported my decision to take time off work; he was just sorry to see me leave. I left with my head held high to begin another phase of my life.

5

Crossing the QLTT Hurdle

One of the undesirable consequences of my resignation was forfeiting the sponsorship of my QLTT qualification. I had no choice but to pay for the exams myself. With barely any savings and no income, the fees put a strain on my finances. The common-sense approach would have been to save up, at least six months' salary, before resigning, but if I had waited that long, I would have talked myself out of my radical decision to leave.

Since I had chosen not to wait, I knew I had to make it work. I calculated my living expenses, including my mortgage, and drastically adjusted my lifestyle. I let out the spare room in my property. The income from the rent covered a sizable portion of my expenses and the rest I drew from my savings.

When I finally told my family, I was grateful and relieved to receive their support even though they did not wholly agree with me. So, I proceeded, without the luxury of relying on others for encouragement and strength. I had to live by my personal philosophy that it is always better to draw strength from one's own identity than it is to rely on external validation.

After a few days at home, the reality of being out of a job hit me hard. I hardly knew what to do with my time, and it felt awkward. I had been accustomed to the routine of waking up early in the morning and going to work for so long, I felt out of my depth without the comfort of my routine. Thankfully, within a week, I snapped out the depressing mood and took steps to implement my plan. I enrolled with a reputable QLTT training provider in London where I was told I had missed a few weeks of lectures. I was tempted to defer at least one of the modules but concluded that it would defeat the sacrifice I had made in quitting my job.

The weeks of preparation were intense. Ten-hour daily studying cycles were the norm. I was not just studying to pass the examinations; I wanted to gain a deep understanding of U.K. laws and regulations and learn how to practically apply them in my career. After the weeks of gruelling study and hard work, I needed a break, but I could not afford a decent holiday. Help came through a friend who invited me for an all-expenses-paid holiday in the U.A.E. It could not have come at a better time. The time away from law books was truly refreshing and I felt invigorated when I returned to my studies a couple of weeks later.

The week of the examinations arrived, along with

unprecedented levels of snowfall and disruptions to travel. At the time, I lived on the outskirts of London time, and had to draw up a contingency plan to arrive at the examination centre on time. I considered all available options and settled on staying in a hotel within a mile of the examination centre in Central London, which a friend of mine offered to pay for. My decision proved to be vital as disruptions to travel due to the adverse weather continued to escalate, and sadly, some of the candidates missed the examination as a result.

As I waited for the exam results to be released, I must have marked my scripts, in my head, a thousand times until I thought my head would explode. Although I had a quiet confidence that I had done enough to pass the examinations, I wanted my performance to be exceptional! Eventually, the results were published, and my results were outstanding. I was delighted my glowing performance, given my late start. My dream of becoming a fully qualified solicitor in England and Wales had finally been fulfilled.

Throughout my career, I had been privileged to be in mentoring relationships that played a vital role in my career progression. My mentor at that time was a director in one of the big four audit firms. We met at a career event that I attended where he was one of the guest speakers. After listening to his speech, I knew he was someone that could support me in my career aspirations. I approached him after the event and was particularly touched by his humility. I had expected him to gently turn down my request but was pleasantly surprised when he accepted.

During one of our meetings, my mentor asked if I had given any thought to my next salary package and how much I would like to earn. His question prompted me to carry out some research and I discovered that I had been underestimating my earning potential as a qualified solicitor in the U.K. I had under-earned for so long that I had subconsciously settled for less than my earning potential. Following my review, I came up with figures that accurately reflected my new status.

6

Launching into the Next Level

Armed with my new qualification, I registered with a handful of carefully selected legal and company secretarial recruitment agencies. I had a target in mind and was only willing to work with people with the gravitas to lead me to my next big opportunity. I recall having a light bulb moment about my CV on my way to an interview at one of the recruitment agencies I registered with. I felt that my CV focused extensively on my achievements and barely expressed my capabilities and personality.

I arrived at the agency with my mind dominated by thoughts of how to bring my personality to life through my CV. I listened half-heartedly as the recruitment consultant described a few suitable roles. I waited for her to stop talking and rather than give my feedback on the roles she had identified, I asked her to do a critical review of my CV. From the look on her face, it was clear that my request had caught her off guard. I quickly followed up my request with an explanation about the thoughts I had about my CV and asked for her advice on CV construction.

Apparently, my direct approach and willingness to acknowledge her expertise impressed her. She confided that in all her years as a consultant, no one had ever asked her for CV advice. She agreed to review my CV and then dedicated over two hours to evaluating each section and transferring all her knowledge and experience about CV writing to me. I left the meeting with a spring in my step. What I did not know then was that, because of that meeting, I would later become a CV expert

Based on my newly acquired knowledge, I spent hours reconstructing my CV until I was confident it accurately reflected my personality and capabilities. I sent the reconstructed CV to the recruitment consultant – she had agreed to review the updated version – and I received a glowing review. I also sent it to some of my professional colleagues and friends and received similar feedback.

I sent the new CV to recruitment consultants, and the calls started rolling in. I shortlisted the interview requests to five mid-senior management roles. There was one interview in particular that I didn't quite have the right experience or technical qualifications for. The recruiters had been impressed with my CV and decided to invite me anyway. I included this particular role in my shortlist more out of curiosity than anything else. I was keen to find out what exactly they found impressive about my CV.

The Interviews and Choosing the Next Level

The interview took place in the meeting rooms of a prestigious hotel in Central London because the company was based in Prague. I responded honestly to their questions and admitted to the aspects of the role that I was not knowledgeable in. At the end of the interview, the senior executive explained to me that even though it was apparent that I was not suitable for the role, they wished to offer me a newly created role. My performance in the interview had convinced them that I would be a valuable addition to their organisation. The role I had applied for was based in Prague and came with an attractive relocation package; however, I was given the opportunity to engage in fresh negotiations for the new role. Although I enjoyed the whole experience, I knew I would be deviating from my path if I accepted the job offer.

After the round of interviews, I ended up with four job offers, all with attractive packages. I narrowed my options down to two: a telecommunications company and an automotive company. After considering both offers, I opted for the telecommunications company even though I had no prior experience whatsoever in the telecommunications industry. The job offer was a dream come true. It ticked the box from a financial, work-life balance and career progression perspective. Interestingly, with the new income, I was able to recoup my lost income for being out of work, within six months.

I would later find out that another candidate that was considered for the role had over seven years of relevant industry experience, but my passion and personality had impressed the interviewers. Also, some knowledge of French was considered essential for the role, but I had no knowledge of French at the time, only the willingness to learn.

A Multi-National Telecomm. Company

I joined a multi-national telecommunications company as Company Secretary for the U.K. region with additional responsibilities that included corporate legal functions. During the second stage of my interview for this role, the interviewer was impressed with what I was proposing to bring into the company, although it sounded too good to be true. With such expectations hanging over me, I was determined to make my mark in the organisation. I was not about to let the organisation or myself down.

I was practically thrown in at the deep end. On my first day, I sat through a six-hour board meeting that left me physically and mentally exhausted. It had been almost a year since I had been in a full-on corporate environment, and I quickly realised that it would require a significant amount of effort and dedication to achieve the level of success I desired. So, I rolled up my sleeves and got to work.

I began by thoroughly reviewing the existing company secretarial processes in the company. I identified the efficiency gaps and rated them according to their level of complexity. Then starting with the least complex, I transformed each process until there was a noticeable improvement in overall efficiency. By tackling the easiest problems first, I scored quick wins and demonstrated my willingness and ability to effect meaningful change.

I signed up for several projects, especially in the areas where I had limited experience. This was my go-to strategy for acquiring the knowledge, experience and skills that I lacked, even if it meant making mistakes along the way. On one of such projects, I was required to advise on a multi-billion financial transaction project which, due to its scale, would usually have been outsourced to external legal counsel. It was thrilling and nerve wrecking at the same time, and I knew there was no room for error.

I spent weeks carrying out in-depth research and frequently used my company secretarial colleagues as a sounding board. I successfully completed this project and others within a few months at the company. With my confidence soaring, I continued to put myself forward to lead multi-million and multi-billion pound projects in the U.K. region.

In my first performance review, I scored 120% out of 100%, having exceeded my target by 20%! I was humbled by this result. I admit that it was a team effort, but it felt good to be part of a very successful team, knowing that the projects I delivered contributed to the collective success of the team.

I proactively expanded the scope of my role through

my willingness to take up more responsibilities, even when it didn't seem the logical thing to do. I found great comfort in the accolades and reviews I was receiving from colleagues and senior management. More satisfying, however, was the sheer feeling of excitement I got from setting my mind on resolving complex challenges and seeing them through to completion.

7

Success is Repeatable

About a year after I joined the multinational telecommunications company, the Head of U.K. central operations invited me into her office and after a brief discussion, promoted me to legal counsel and company secretary of the U.K. division. I was totally unprepared for her announcement. I had set a three-year target for my first promotion and had neither requested nor solicited this promotion. I was truly grateful for the promotion and felt it was recognition and reward for my hard work and contributions to the organisation.

Several years down the line, the story has not changed. I am a valued member of the senior management team and I continue to represent the U.K. division of the business globally and advise on wider corporate projects. I have survived several redundancies in the company.

After more than ten years of working in the U.K., I

have unequivocally dispelled my friend's projections that I was likely to end up with shattered dreams.

Given my slow start and average performance early on in life, I have succeeded against all the odds. I was not prepared to settle for mediocrity; with determination and conviction, I took the bold step to rewrite my story. To an undiscerning mind, my successes may appear to be sheer luck. But I did not achieve my career aspirations by waiting for luck to bring the right circumstances my way. I took deliberate, progressive and incremental steps that ensured success in my career and changed my story dramatically.

I am not saying I was always in control of all the factors that contributed to my success; there were undoubtedly factors beyond my control, but to the extent that I could influence circumstances, I gave it my best shot.

One significant factor that contributed to my success and took care of the elements beyond my control is my faith in God. It sustained me during the times when it felt like my efforts were not yielding the desired results.

I do not believe that success or failure is accidental. Neither do I believe that past failures, disappointments and disadvantages determine your destination in life. Within every individual lies an inherent ability to steer the course of their life in the direction they desire. Success is attainable, regardless of your beginning. But it will not happen by chance. It will happen because you take deliberate action and apply winning strategies.

In the rest of this book, I will unveil to you the strategies and tools I applied that brought me outstanding success in my career. I urge you to keep an open mind.

PART II

Principles, Strategies & Tools

About Part II

*I*n Part 1, I shared my story as an immigrant who rose through the ranks to become a solicitor and company secretary in the U.K. Despite my somewhat slow and tumultuous start in life, my fervent desire to succeed coupled with the right principles, strategies, and tools allowed me to beat the odds and surpass every expectation.

In this part of the book, I'll be sharing some of these principles, strategies & tools for success I used, though sometimes unconsciously, with you. Over time, I have discovered that these same principles, strategies & tools apply not only to Career Progression but in fact, can be applied to any goal you are reaching out for.

8

The Image Inside You is Everything

*I*t all starts with an image! Let me give you two definitions of "image" I have come across.

'a physical likeness or representation of a person, animal, or thing, photographed, painted, sculptured, or otherwise made visible.'

a 'mental representation, idea or conception.

Without a clear image of your end goal, whether it is something you want or who you see yourself becoming, it is unlikely you will recognise the goal when you achieve it. Imagine you get on a train without having a clear destination in mind, any stop could be your destination. Unfortunately, any stop you get off at may not be a stop you like. Having an image helps you evaluate your progress towards a desired goal. I once read that, 'To the person who does not know where he wants to go, there is no favourable wind.'

Once you have an image of what your goal looks like, take the next step. Write it down. Writing has a way of crystallising the ideas in your mind and giving you clarity. Writing stimulates your mind and inspires thought processes that support and enhance the image. Also, a documented final image helps you measure progress.

Although I had a slow start in my early years, the moment I created a mental picture of where I wanted to be, my life took on new meaning and direction. I became intentional with every step I took. I began to channel my time, energy and resources towards achieving the picture I could, clearly, see inside me. The image was indelibly etched in my mind that it helped me avoid distractions.

9

Sharpen Your Focus

Nowadays, we are constantly bombarded with an avalanche of information and options. This makes it an arduous task to focus on and follow a set path to a logical conclusion. Focus means, 'to concentrate,' 'to direct one's attention and effort,' 'the clear and sharply defined condition of an image.' To lack focus is to waste time, energy and precious resources. Without focus, you most likely will engage in activities that are not bringing you closer to your goal. I once heard someone say, "Activity does not need to equate to results." Without focus, you will engage in activities but not have the results your desire

When I arrived in England, there were so many career options I could have settled for. Career options were constantly being thrown at me by friends, colleagues and peers who meant well and wanted me to succeed. However, as much as I appreciated their kindness, I knew I had to stay focused on my goal.

Maintaining focus does not necessarily mean you cannot do other things during the period when you are reaching for your goal. The nature of your target and the length of time required to achieve it will determine the boundaries beyond which you start to lose focus. Some goals are for a brief period while others take longer. For instance, one of my goals is to run in a marathon and complete the course. As much as I would like to achieve that goal sooner rather than later, I realise that I will need to build up my stamina and energy over a sustained period to achieve it.

I hope you realise that when I talk about focus, I am not referring to the process you take to actualise your goal. Focussing on the goal and the processes to attaining the goal are very different things. For example, You may want to go from city A to city B with city B being your goal. However, the process of getting to City B will depend on the mode of transport you chose to go for. Focus is about keeping your eye on the destination but remaining flexible in your choice of how to get there. Some people lose focus by paying too much attention to the "how".

Remember, when I first got to the UK, my main goal was to become a practicing company secretary and solicitor. However, as I considered options, I discovered the conventional route was not right for me. I researched other ways that could help me achieve my goal and decided to go through the professional qualification route, sat the required exams and achieved my goal. Even though there were other options that appeared more logical and maybe even easier, they would not have taken me to my destination.

You need to be careful here though. If the challenges of going through the process are too onerous, you may change your mind so, write your goals down and evaluate the different routes that will get you there and choose the path that's right for you.

10

Have Values

*O*ur values are the belief systems that underpin our actions. The way we live and conduct ourselves is an indicator of our value system. Your value system usually drives the reason for your goals. Your value system helps you answer the "why?" question. Our values define how we live, what we say, where we go, and they permeate every aspect of our lives

To attain success and personal happiness in life, your values must direct you towards fulfilling your dreams. When actions correlate with values, they bring a deep sense of fulfilment. For example, excellence and hard work are values that are important to me. As a result, I always apply myself diligently to whatever work I take on. This value system was a significant contributing factor in accomplishing my goal of landing a company secretarial role in multi-national telecommunications company. If developing the right level of expertise is important to you, then you will find it easy to spend your resources looking for the right minds to nurture you. If needed, you will engage the services of experts.

Your values help to define the ethical boundaries you will not be willing to cross. They also define how quickly you may give up when things get tough. Completed actions are what make goal attainment possible.

A misalignment between your values and actions often lead to frustration. Therefore, it is important to identify our values and examine our actions to ensure they match up.

11

Manage Time Well

*T*here is a wise old saying that says, "time is the most valuable thing a person can spend". This could not be truer. You can predict a person's outcome if you know how they invest their time. Time and value are two sides of the same coin. They travel in the same direction. What you value determines the amount of time you will spend cultivating it.

Let's say two students are studying for a finance degree at university. Both have similar backgrounds and exposure, and both aspire to be finance professionals. One decides to spend his school holidays gaining some work experience, as an unpaid intern, in a financial institution while the other secures a holiday job in a retail outlet with pay and benefits. At the end of their degree programme, the unpaid intern would have acquired the relevant experience in finance even though he may not have made as much money as the one that worked for pay and benefits. The other would also have gained some work experience, but irrelevant to his area of discipline.

Obviously, this is a very simplistic scenario but imagine that both of them applied for roles in a financial organisation – the original goal. One would have the required financial experience and would be more likely to get the role.

Recognising the value of time in utilising the opportunities available can be the deciding factor between success and failure. It can make the difference between good and great. Managing your time effectively allows you employ time as an advantage, not a liability. Time management is an indispensable tool for success. It is an invaluable asset that is optimised by successful people.

12

Is Your Mind Set?

*Y*our mindset is the way you approach or react to a situation. I came across some research done by world-renowned Stanford University psychologist Carol Dweck from decades of research on achievement and success. Of her conclusions, there were two points that stuck out for me. 1.) the view you adopt in life profoundly affects your outcomes and can determine your level of success in life and 2.) The identification of two mindsets namely, the fixed mindset and the growth mindset.

People with a fixed mindset believe that traits such as intelligence and talents are set and cannot be developed. They also believe that talent alone creates success. People with a growth mindset, on the other hand, believe that ability can be developed through hard work, and that intelligence and talent are only the starting point.

This view encourages learning and creates an

enabling atmosphere for the accomplishment of one's goals. A growth mindset opens you up to the belief that your abilities can be cultivated through your efforts. People with a growth mindset believe that a person's potential is unlimited and not fully known, and that it is impossible to foresee what can be accomplished with years of dedication passion, practice and training. A fixed mindset focuses on limitations, while a growth mindset focuses on possibilities.

These questions can help you determine if you have a growth or fixed mindset.

> *Do you believe that your abilities and talents are set and cannot be improved upon?*
>
> *Do your beliefs give you the perfect excuse for underachievement?*
>
> *Do you readily find fault with everything and everyone else but yourself?*

An individual that answers 'Yes' to these questions has a fixed mindset and is therefore unlikely to realise their full potential. Research shows that virtually all successful people have adopted a growth mindset at some point. I have also found it this to be true in my journey.

While in primary school, I had an unpleasant teacher who managed to instil the idea in me that I could not handle mathematics and I embraced this as truth for a very long time. As a result, I stopped trying to excel in mathematics and focused my energy on other subjects like English Language and English literature. After registering for the ICSA qualifying modules, I discovered that one of the requisite modules was corporate financial management, which requires a degree of maths skills. My initial response was that the math element would make it difficult for me to pass that module. Although I attended lectures and exposed myself to the necessary knowledge, I could not shake my belief that I did not have the ability to do well in the module.

As you may have rightly predicted, I failed that course. I failed by only 15 marks. Seeing how close I was to the pass mark sent a chill down my spine. What I needed to pass the module was not as much as I thought. Had I challenged the mindset with a bit more effort, I would have made it. The fear of maths led me to focus on the less challenging modules but I chose to respond positively to the failure by learning from it. I re-registered for the course and this time round, I was more intentional about my desire to pass. I attended lectures, practised the exercises and prepared with determination and focus. This made all the difference and I realised that the course was not as difficult as I believed. When the results were published, I had one of the best scores in the module. This taught me a very profound lesson about mindset and how it affects our endeavours.

I also struggled with my weight. For as long as I can remember, I have wanted to be slim. But each time I tried to lose weight, I would fall short of my desired dress size. One of the convenient excuses I adopted was that I have big bones and would always be on the plus side regardless of diet, exercise or a healthy lifestyle. This excuse was so deeply entrenched in my mind that I stopped trying to lose weight altogether. However, once I identified and addressed the limiting mindset, I became more open to the possibility of losing weight and I took on the challenge. Five months into my weight loss programme, I had lost more than half of my original weight.

13

Is Brand "You" Intact?

The last time you were at the grocery store, did you notice how many times you chose branded items over the plain-looking store brand, even though they were more expensive? Have you asked yourself why people choose Kellogg's corn flakes over the store brand, or shop for clothes in designer stores instead of the clothes section of a supermarket? It's the power of branding! We live in a global village where only the people who recognise and harness the immense power of branding will thrive and succeed in their endeavours.

Branding is everything. Branding can determine the success or failure of your products or services. The good news is that everyone has a chance to stand out, a chance to make a statement, a chance to be distinguished. Big organisations spend endless budgets and time reinforcing their brand because they understand its value.

Do you realise you are a brand? The world reads you more than you can imagine. How are you promoting your brand? Do you have a clear message that communicates your brand effectively? One of the fundamental principles that you need to establish is a unique selling point (USP). You can only develop your USP when you see yourself as different, outstanding and unique. What differentiates you from your colleagues or a million people that are doing the same thing as you? What do the people that use your product or service say about it? Do they even recognise your impact?

You can transcend the narrow boundaries that try to contain your potential.

Professional services consultants exploit this power of personal branding. They usually have nothing but soft assets with which they solve problems for their clients. Their investments in personal training and development lead to new expertise with which they create value for their clients.

So, think about brand "you." What benefits are derived from you? Do people attribute the value of punctuality to you? Do they consider you as a problem solver? Are you associated with foresight? Are you linked with integrity? There are many more questions I could ask here but the key point to remember is that your personal brand is not a function of your job title or position, but rather of your disposition. It is the value people attribute to your personality. Personal branding is not only for professionals or senior executives. Personal branding should apply to all.

To develop your brand, I usually suggest using well-known models like the Strengths, Weakness, Opportunities & Threats (SWOT) analysis which helps you identify strengths you should develop greater expertise in, weaknesses that need strengthening or avoiding altogether, opportunities you may want to take advantage of and threats that need to be mitigated.

You need to play to your strengths and not your weaknesses. Let people know what you are good at before you use your mouth to run down yourself by talking about your weakness in the presence of those who are interested in your strengths. Make yourself visible to the people that matter. For example, if you are trying to move into management, how visible are you to those who are already in management? Do you run away from volunteering for high profile projects for the fear of failure? When you do very good work, do senior management know your involvement in the work?

Let me finish with this point. Personal branding is not just about how you look, although presentation is important. The real power behind your brand is the quality of your product or service, as well as your ability to secure the trust of your clients. Your brand must be backed with substance.

14

Discipline

Discipline is a foundational principle for success. It involves training yourself to identify and stick to certain ways of living consistent with your value system and the objectives you want to achieve. I am yet to meet or hear of a successful person who is not disciplined. Without discipline it is difficult to adopt most of the principles presented in this book.

We live in a time when many instant pleasures are competing for our attention, and it is very easy to get distracted from the things that are important. Discipline cuts across thoughts, words and actions.

We are daily bombarded with many things that could represent a distraction. I came across the result of a study sometime ago that suggested that adults make an average of thirty-five thousand decisions a day. This level of decision-making is the recipe for mental exhaustion. We need to identify our priorities and develop a structure that allows us focus on them. Develop the habits that cultivate the things you want to be good at.

From box sets to social media to news, we daily have many opportunities to get distracted. It is pertinent to identify your priorities and develop a structure that allows you focus on your priorities. Discipline cannot be exercised without an understanding of the value of time. There are only twenty-four hours in a day; recognising that every minute of that 24-hour cycle matters will help you train yourself to spend your time on important tasks.

Living a disciplined life is not as hard as it seems. Everyone applies discipline in at least one area of their life. I believe a key challenge is knowing how to apply discipline to every area of life. For instance, some people can maintain a healthy lifestyle but struggle to apply the same level of discipline to their career. One way to develop discipline is to focus on the desired outcome. For example, volunteering to spend unpaid hours on a work project may not be convenient, but focusing on the desired outcome of increased visibility will motivate you to stick with it.

I encourage you to evaluate how you spend your time from the moment you wake up until you go to sleep. Make a note of the activities you engage in, even the most mundane ones, and how long you spend on them. This will help you determine how productive your time is.

Remember, what you spend most of your time on is

indicative of your true values.

Personally, I hardly watch TV and I am very strict about how much time I spend on social media. Those are two activities that can drain my time and I put a tight rein on how much time I spend on them. There are good things on social media and it can be a good platform to promote yourself and raise your visibility.

However, it is important to be intentional about how you spend your time on it.

15

Don't Confuse Your Personality With Your Behaviour

*T*his is one of the most challenging areas for people to unravel. Often, we fail to distinguish between personality and behaviour. Personality is *'the combination of characteristics or qualities that form an individual's distinctive character'*. Behaviour, on the other hand, is *'the way in which one acts or conducts oneself, especially towards others'*[1]. The ability to control your personality and your behaviour effectively and use them to your advantage will bring you closer to your goals.

People tend to believe that certain jobs and roles are suited for certain personality types. While this line of thought may be, generally, correct, there are also exceptions. For example, it is believed that jobs in leadership and professional sales are better suited to extroverts. Susan Cain in her book, "*Quiet – The*

---
1 Oxford Dictionary.

Power of Introverts in a World That Can't Stop Talking" introduced a fresh perspective as to why this assertion may not necessarily be true. She suggested that introverts can be just as successful in leadership as extroverts, but without all the flurry. Introverts can exhibit extroverted behaviours as necessary to achieve their outcomes. Consequently, it is possible to transcend personality-based limitations by identifying the required behavioural traits for a given task.

In my case, I spent time researching and identifying the required skillset, knowledge and gravitas for a company secretary that advises board members and senior management. I intentionally worked on exhibiting those behaviours, even though I was not naturally inclined towards them.

Many organisations have a culture that is entrenched in their values, and they take this into account when hiring. To progress your career, you need to understand and align yourself with the culture of your organisation and the behavioural traits associated with that culture. This is one of the strategies for promotion, especially at senior management level. I am puzzled when I come across people who complain about stagnancy in their career but are stuck in their ways and refuse to play the part required for promotion. Organisations are more likely to promote an individual that portrays a good understanding of the company culture and exhibits the right behaviour, even if they are not as sound in technical knowledge.

Humans are complex and multifaceted. We can be different people in different situations without losing our personal identity. This is, perhaps, why someone who seems domineering and assertive in the workplace is amiable at home. Such a person is only rising to the demand of each function and acting accordingly. However, few people recognise this skill and use it to their advantage.

I urge you to reflect on the required skills and qualities for your target goal and examine whether you are acting the part. Think about who you need to become for that goal. Your promotion to that next level you desire may depend on it.

16

Competency: The Core of Success

We should always aim to be at the top of whatever field we find ourselves in. To be regarded as an expert is an indispensable tool for career success. Customers come to you because they perceive you to have a product or are better at creating a service they require. In one of my previous roles, I gained specialised knowledge after conducting a due diligence exercise on more than two hundred and fifty companies.

Ericsson in his research on "The role of deliberate practice in the acquisition of expertise" alluded to the fact that it takes up to ten years or ten thousand hours to gain expertise that leads to prominence. This is, on average, four hours of work over and beyond regular working hours. A feat that can only be realistically achieved if started early enough in life. Great sportsmen and International performers spend hours daily practising and refining their skills.

Geoffrey Cohen in his book "Talent is Overrated" described deliberate practice as the practice that is performed repetitively over time and specifically targeted at improving performance. For me, this not only involved improving the skills I already had, but also extending the range. The due diligence exercise I conducted helped me develop skills such as knowledge acquisition, research and analytical skills. The work itself was very challenging. There were times when it seemed I had taken three steps forward only to go five steps backwards or times when the finishing line was just in sight, I got presented with fresh information and evidence that took me back to the initial stages of the research. My persistence paid off in the end. Many of the competencies and skills that I deployed in subsequent roles, even in other companies, were acquired during that exercise.

While the rewards are significant, the journey to becoming a subject matter expert can be lonely. It is mentally demanding and exerting and, of course, not always fun. In most cases, it will involve applying rigour over protracted periods. As the saying goes, "if it were fun and easy, more people would have towed the path."

Competency is not a destination. It's a journey

After I qualified as a solicitor and company secretary, I recognised the need to keep my knowledge relevant and up to date. A degree or professional qualification is the foundation for the acquisition of practical knowledge and skills. The advent of technology has revolutionised our world. Our disciplines and fields of study are increasingly influenced by technology driving the pace at which new knowledge is derived. We, therefore, need to apply ourselves and continuously seek out means to keep our minds updated.

In my career, I have attended several courses and seminars organised by law firms. I have also kept up to date with developments through subscriptions to relevant publications. In one of my previous teams, each member was required to lead presentations on new and updated insights, during training meetings. I committed about two to three hours daily, after work to researching and preparing for these presentations but long after the training, the knowledge has stayed with me.

Knowledge acquisition can be likened to the process of refining precious commodities. First, drilling takes place, usually for years, to find the material in its raw form. Then comes the process of refining, which can be long and unpleasant but produces beautiful precious stones in the end. Likewise, you must drill deep and keep refining your knowledge and skills until you become an authority in your field.

Companies such as Apple and Google have billions of dollars in the reserves; not because there are insufficient projects to spend them on, but they are seeking unique individuals with phenomenal innovative capabilities. Human capital is one of the scarcest resources of our time. Innovation will flow from the right human capital.

Be an expert in your field but spread your knowledge

As a solicitor and company secretary that supports businesses operating in diverse industries, I had to be a bit of 'Jack of all trades' and understand the mechanisms of areas such as finance, IT, human resources, treasury and tax. I spent time with colleagues to understand these areas, and how they support a business in delivering its objectives. This empowered me to advise the business more effectively. Secondary domain knowledge involves understanding wider issues affecting the business, beyond your area of specialism. I believe it is the extra-factor that can set you apart from your peers.

17

Success: Myth or Reality

Success principles are failure-proof. They will work in any part of the world, provided you apply them effectively. I could relocate to the United States, Canada or the Middle East, apply the principles that I have learnt over the years and the results would be similar. Remember, success is repeatable.

Sometimes, we are too scared to aim high and end up not setting stretching goals for ourselves. For me, although I had a clear picture of what I wanted to accomplish, I did not mention them for fear of being mocked but now, having gone through the journey, I see how pervasive beliefs can also shape our thinking and prevent us from reaching for great heights. For example, many believe that extraordinary talent, social influence or an excellent degree from an ivy league school is a prerequisite for success. While some of these enabling factors do enhance your chances of succeeding, I will certainly not agree that success cannot be achieved outside of them. In fact, relying on your degree or connections can limit your creative abilities and generate a sense of complacency or entitlement.

I certainly do not wish to undermine the importance of innate capabilities; talent, retentive memory, high intelligence, social advantage and influence. These are all advantageous. However, without practice and consistent application of success principles, they may not translate into greatness. This should be good news that encourages us to break the mental barriers that have limited us and restricted success to a selected few. But more importantly, it should reinforce the belief that there is no excuse for failure.

Your success or failure is directly related to the level of your effort and not necessarily any mitigating external factors. You don't need to be an expert at so many things, or have all enabling factors mentioned above to be a success in life.

PART III

A Call To Action

About Part III

I have, so far, in this book, shared my story and the principles, strategies, and tools that enabled me to achieve my career ambitions. Here, I focus on helping you create and chart your own roadmap to career success.

Success is not without its challenges, and I have had my own fair share of them. However, there were a few key questions I asked myself during those challenging times that helped to streamline my efforts and increase my effectiveness. I will be asking you the same questions with the hope of helping you achieve a similar outcome to mine.

19

Have You Met "You"?

Self-discovery – the process of gaining *insight* into who you are and what you are capable of - is a catalyst for lasting success. It played a crucial role in helping me achieve career success. It is important for you to know who you are, that you understand your personality, your strengths, your weaknesses and your passions. Self-discovery is a continuum and will evolve as you progress through different stages of life.

Underpinning self-discovery is that moment when you become aware of the real you. You become aware of what you are capable of and develop a resolve to be better than your current state. Getting to this state is crucial to your journey because it is the point at which you intentionally seek out tools and resources that will help to compliment your uniqueness.

It was when I reached this point that I identified

the skills that I needed to develop for success. I focussed on my strengths and honed the skills that complimented them. I stopped trying to wear too many hats and instead, focused on showcasing the skills that highlighted my strengths. This approach significantly reduced time and energy wastage on irrelevant activities.

Sometimes, life brings circumstances and challenges that temporarily impair our natural abilities and strengths. During those trying times, many people tend to wrongly believe that they should be defined by those circumstances. Holding on to that sort of belief actually stifles self-discovery and self-actualisation because the setbacks and comebacks you experience in life are good indicators of your qualities, strengths and temperament.

It took me two decades to not only discover myself but to get to a place where I enthusiastically celebrate and nurture my identity. If I had allowed the challenges I faced in the past to define my abilities and future prospects, I would have put a firm lid on the vast pool of possibilities that awaited me in the future.

Discovering *you* can happen in many different ways. You will need to strip away the layers of past experiences and people's opinions that have moulded your life over the years to get to you so you can identify the likes, dislikes, passion, natural abilities that you are most comfortable and confident with. This is by no means a quick formula for self-discovery. It is an ongoing process of deep contemplation to progressively unveil the different aspects of your inner self. You may not get answers immediately, but you will be surprised at what you discover as the layers start to peel off.

To discover *you*, you should also ask people you trust who can tell you the truth about how you come across to others. Ask them to describe you using adjectives. Other people interpret you through your words and actions while you tend to interpret yourself through your thoughts. Usually, there is a wide gap between these two perspectives. A note of caution here, while it may be beneficial to listen to people you respect and trust, particularly people who can help you identify blind spots, it is still essential that you take full responsibility for your actions and decisions, knowing that they will affect you more than anyone else.

20

Who Influences You?

*I*nfluence is a very compelling concept. One Dictionary[1] describes it as *"the act or power of producing an effect without apparent exertion of force or direct exercise of command."* Whoever influences you has a measure of control over your life that you may not even be aware of.

You should evaluate your life and reflect on some of the decisions you have made to this point. Taking a passive approach when making important decisions and allowing people to dictate the path we travel can have a significant effect on our outcomes.

When I made up my mind to relocate to the United Kingdom, I had a very bleak picture painted for me by well-meaning friends and family. Had I taken their view into consideration, I would not be where I am today. Even though there was a chance that my strategy may not have yielded the outcomes I

---
[1] Merriam-Webster.com

desired, and the bleak views painted could have become my reality. Taking the leap was a risk worth taking.

At every critical point in my journey, I always took the time to, deeply, reflect on my decisions and choices before I made them. I knew I could not afford to blame anyone but myself for the resulting outcomes. I had no right to blame anyone for whatever happened to me in life. This belief heightened my determination to not only make the right decisions but to stand firm by my decisions irrespective of the challenges that I encountered along the way.

Take ownership for your decisions. Be sure you are making your decision for the right reasons to avoid so you avoid the propensity to be unwilling to take responsibility for your outcomes, particularly, if negative. It is so easy to blame everyone else but yourself for your mistakes and bad choices. Acknowledge your mistakes and apply the necessary corrective measures. When you maintain a strong sense of responsibility for your life, you can be intentional about your personal growth.

It is time to take the front wheel of your life and steer it towards your desired destination. Think about some of your plans and the decisions you need to make to achieve them. Write them down and review each one with your end goal in mind. Document the reasons behind your decisions. If they don't give you the desired outcomes, at least, you will have gained the right knowledge to help inform better choices.

21

Do You Understand Ambition and Goals?

*Y*our ambition and goals go hand in hand. Always ensure you are pursuing the right dreams for the right reasons. When ambition is fuelled by negative emotions, the goal, even when achieved, will ultimately lead to dissatisfaction and emptiness within.

What are your goals and ambitions?

I can often tell, when I engage in conversations with people, if they are ambitious or not. Their narrative gives them away. Success hardly ever happens by accident. It takes calculated and deliberate action. An individual who does not have high aspirations cannot expect to experience greatness! Likewise, the person with big dreams is more likely to defy conventions and traditions, and be ingenious in their quest for greatness.

It makes no difference if your dream seems achievable or not. All of the advancements we see in the world today were dreamt up by innovators and were once considered impossible. Sometimes, those dreams may not be achieved by you, but your contributions can serve as the foundation for another individual or generation to build upon.

Every invention that is enjoyed today such as tablets, mobile phones, aeroplanes, computers etc. started off as someone's dream. Your dreams have the potential to transform the world beyond your imagination.

I have many big dreams. One of which is to inspire and influence millions of people to achieve their dreams and be the best they can be. I believe some of my dreams will be achieved in my lifetime, but there are others that I sense my role will be to inspire other people to go on and pursue theirs. The most important thing is to identify your dreams and take the right steps towards realising them.

Remember though, that as you reach for your goals, you will probably fail at least once as you try to accomplish them. The question is, 'What will you do with that failure?' Will it inspire you to keep going until you succeed, or will it stir up negative emotions that end up setting you back. Failure is an invaluable part of success. The fact that you failed does not make you a failure. You need to separate your experience of failure from who you are. In my own experiences, I have observed an event of failure on the path to success makes the achievement more compelling and rewarding. Failure has a way of keeping you humble and grounded and will make you value success even more. Without an element of failure, it is possible for one to get overconfident and not truly appreciate the process that success demands.

Why do you want to achieve your goals and ambitions?

People can usually identify their goals and ambitions, but struggle to articulate the *why*. Why do you want that position, contract, innovation, partnership or acquisition? A simple statement opener such as '*so I can have a better….*' or '*so I can be a better…*' can help you answer this question.

Knowing the *why* is a strong indication of the lengths you will be prepared to go to achieve them. As a matter of fact, it is a strong indicator of whether you will achieve the goal or not.

I was asked the same question when I decided to complete this book after unsuccessful attempts, and it prompted a time of sober reflection. Why do you want to write this book? In answering this question, I discovered that my why connected deeply with my dream and insatiable desire for inspiring and bringing out the best in people. Taking the time to uncover your why will increase your chances of achieving your goal. It will also help you distinguish between the goals that are worth pursuing and those that are not. When you identify your *why*, your desire to pursue your goals will either increase or wane. If your *why* is strong enough, it will compel you, in spite of the challenges you experience, to realise your goal.

So you have set your goals and ambitions and have started executing them. Have you paused to imagine the emotions and feelings that you will experience when you finally achieve them? It would be great if you plan a well-deserved treat when you accomplish your goal. The reward of achieving your goals should also serve as a motivating factor. Make a decision to reward yourself when you achieve each step of your goals. After all, you worked hard for it!

How much do you desire your ambition?

The average person has a myriad of dreams and ambitions, but only a fraction of people live to see them fulfilled. How much do you desire to accomplish those goals and ultimately your dreams? Does the desire consume you enough to provoke action and personal sacrifice? You cannot fully achieve your goals without the right level of desire. The price of success is often high. There will be times when you feel you are not making progress. Life will throw many challenges at you and only the deepest conviction that will keep you focused.

It is more than likely that you will need to adopt a graded approach to achieving your goals. For instance, one of my goals is to run the London Marathon. Although I have nursed this dream for many years, my commitment to it is nowhere near my commitment to excel in my career and to inspire people. If I had to make a choice between tasks related to these two areas, the tasks relating to excellence in career and inspiring people would always take precedence. If your desire is not strong enough, you will not fight valiantly for that dream, and the slightest challenge will, most likely, veer you off course.

What are you doing about it?

The easiest part of your journey to the fulfilment of your dream is making the resolution and the plans. The real work getting yourself to act on your plans. An important action strategy is seeking the right help for the areas you have limited knowledge and skills.

I sought professional help with CV writing, interview preparation and personal branding, something the SWOT analysis tool helped with. It equips you with the knowledge you need to harness your strengths and convert them into expertise, seize your opportunities, mitigate or deter your threats and address your weaknesses. An overall evaluation of these four critical aspects will help you design the right strategy and support structure for your goals.

When are you going to act on it?

My final question to you is perhaps the most important of all. After all, procrastination is one of the greatest reasons for underachievement. The best plans and strategy are worthless without taking the actions required to bring them to reality.

It is very easy to set goals, but until you start taking deliberate steps towards them, you are unlikely to realise them. Our achievements are primarily birthed by the actions we took years, months, weeks and days ago. Taking action today and not waiting until tomorrow distinguishes the outliers from the spectators.

PART IV

Your Personal Action Plan

About Part IV

This section outlines a Personal Action Plan (PAP) for each of the principles, strategies and tools we have talked about. The PAP will help you break your goal down into smaller, more easily achievable steps and identify the actions required for success at each stage.

It has been said that making a right decision is the first step on the road to success. Are you ready to make your own life-changing decision and begin your journey?

1. Creating your story

Your story is one of your greatest recipes for success, but it is often overlooked. There are treasures in your story that could become stimulants for your success. Your setbacks and your comebacks are powerful experiences that you can draw strength from and replicate as you move towards your goals. The greater the challenges you encounter, the more compelling your success story becomes.

Reflection

Think about your past up to your present point and summarise your story in a few pages.

- *What are your greatest challenges?*
- *How did you overcome them?*
- *What were your successes?*
- *What would you like the conclusion of your story to look or sound like?*

Action point

- *Write down your desired conclusion of your story, particularly in line with your goals.*
- *Identify your current strengths that lend into your goals.*
- *Identify the skills, training or knowledge required*

to achieve your goals.

- *Identify the areas of your life you need to develop.*
- *Set your goals in order of priority and start with the one that resonates with you the most. Attempting to take on too much can be overwhelming.*

2. Sharpening your focus

The essence of focus is to keep your attention on your goal and maintain momentum, even in the face of challenges.

Reflection

- *What activities are you currently engaged in?*
- *Which of those activities are adding value to your goals, and to what degree?*
- *Which ones are not? Is it necessary to continue them, or can they be deferred or discontinued?*

Action point

- *Identify your present and imminent activities.*
- *Create a table for all these activities in order of priority and relevance to your goals.*
- *Make a realistic assessment of the activities that lend into your goals and focus only on the most impactful activities, so that you are not overstretched.*

3. Goals and processes

The goal is the end and not the process. The process is what gets you to the goal. Do not be overly fixated on the process at the expense of the goal. Finding creative and unconventional ways of achieving that goal may be the ingenuity element that will help you achieve your goal.

Reflection

- *Have you decided on the right strategy for achieving your goals?*
- *Is the strategy realistic and attainable in your current circumstances?*
- *Is there room for flexibility?*
- *Are there other options that could achieve the same outcome?*

Action point

- *Prepare a course of action for achieving your goals, paying more attention to the end goal.*
- *Ensure that your course of action is flexible and where possible, build a reasonable contingency plan.*
- *Review your course of action frequently as well as your contingency plan.*

4. Have values

Your priorities should point you in the direction of your values. You cannot nurture what you do not value.

Reflection

- *Do you have values and core beliefs regarding the different aspects of your life?*
- *Do you take those values seriously?*
- *Does your lifestyle correspond with your values?*
- *Are your values consistent with your goals?*

Action point

- *Spend time reflecting on your values.*
- *Take deliberate steps to correspond your lifestyle and habits with your values?*
- *Take steps to bridge any gaps between your priorities and your values.*

5. Manage time well

Time and value travel in a similar direction. Doing the right thing is not complete without the complementary factor of time.

Reflection

- *How do you spend your time?*
- *Do you have a habit of keeping to time?*
- *Do you often find yourself procrastinating?*
- *What would people say about your ability to keep to time and meeting deadlines?*

Action point

- *Keep a time management diary and see how well you measure against the targets you set for yourself.*
- *Set one target for yourself to complete an activity and ensure you complete it within the time you allocate.*

6. Is your mind set?

Your viewpoint on life significantly affects your outcomes. You either have a fixed or growth mindset.

Reflection

- *Do you think your talent can be improved upon?*
- *Do you feel limited in areas where you are untalented?*
- *Would you be willing to acquire skills in areas you are not familiar with or not talented?*
- *Do you dwell more on your limitations than your abilities?*

Action point

- *Identify your talents and compare them with someone who was originally thought to be untalented in that area but has developed their skill to world-class.*
- *Identify two new skills that you would like to acquire before the end of the year.*
- *Challenge yourself to gather information on how you can acquire or improve necessary skills, and then take action.*

7. Is brand "you" intact?

Your brand is the subtle message that communicates who you are without you speaking. You cannot rise above your brand.

Reflection

- *Think about the activities that you engage in; how do you do the things you do?*
- *What differentiates you from millions of other people that engage in the same activity?*
- *Do your personal branding tools – CV, marketing brochure, website, blog etc., reflect your personal brand effectively?*
- *Is it compelling enough to give you an advantage?*

Action point

- *Identify your uniqueness and what sets you apart from others doing the same thing as you.*
- *Set a 3 to 6 month period to develop your uniqueness.*
- *Identify a your personal branding platform such as your CV, website, brochure, blog etc., and work on communicating your unique advantages in a compelling way through it?*

8. Discipline

Discipline is the backbone of any significant achievement. A degree of sacrifice is required to stick to our choices.

Reflection

- *Think about the options that are available to you on a daily basis.*

- *Think about the choices that you make from those options.*

- *How many of these choices directly or indirectly connect to your goals?*

Action point

- *Identify two habits that feed into your goal that you would like to cultivate. For instance, read one book a week.*

- *Identify the other options that are competing for the time you should spend cultivating those habits. For example, spending prolonged time on the phone.*

- *Set a relevant time frame within which you would like to cultivate the habit.*

- *Make deliberate choices to engage in the activities that you are trying to develop into a habit.*

9. Evaluating your personality and behaviour

We are complex and multifaceted. We have the capacity to be different people in different situations without losing our identities. Your personality should not stop you from exhibiting the behaviours necessary to fulfil your goals.

Reflection

- *Think about your temperament and some of your qualities.*
- *Think about the different roles and functions that you occupy.*
- *Do you sometimes have to exhibit certain behaviours that contradict your personality?*

Action point

- *Identify two habits that feed into your goal and you Identify the competencies and behaviours required for one of your goals.*
- *Determine whether you currently exhibit the relevant behaviours. If not, practise those behaviours until you can naturally act the part.*

10. Building competency

You need to acquire the right skills, whether soft or hard, to accomplish your goals. Skills acquisition and proficiency can make up for lack of innate talent. Likewise, talent should not be an excuse for lack of skills acquisition and deliberate practice.

Reflection

- *Identify the various skills you currently possess that are relevant to your goals.*
- *How would you rate your ability on these skills?*
- *Identify the skills gaps between you and your goals.*
- *What can you do to bridge those gaps?*

Action point

- *Conduct an assessment of your skills level and benchmark it against market practice or professional standards to determine your proficiency.*
- *If you require more training or experience draw up an action plan to help you acquire them.*
- *Set up a time frame within which this needs to be completed.*

Lightning Source UK Ltd.
Milton Keynes UK
UKHW041810071019
351164UK00001B/2/P